The Future of
a Village

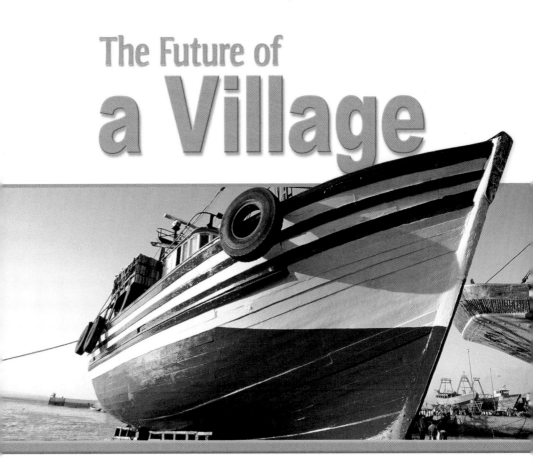

Rob Waring, *Series Editor*

HEINLE
CENGAGE Learning

Australia • Brazil • Japan • Korea • Mexico • Singapore • Spain • United Kingdom • United States

Words to Know

This story is set in Northwest Africa. It happens in Morocco, in the village of Essaouira [ɛsəwɪərə].

 A Fishing Village. Read the paragraph. Label the items in the picture with the underlined words. Then answer the questions.

Essaouira is a very old village near the Atlantic Ocean. It's a fishing **port** and many of the local people are fishermen. Most fishermen go out in a small fishing boat every day. They catch fish and sell them. Fishing has always been important in Essaouira. However, today fishing and boat building are not the only businesses here. Groups of **tourists** are also coming to this interesting village. They come to enjoy the town and its history – and spend money.

1. Which definition best describes '**port**'?
   a. a place by the sea where boats arrive and leave
   b. an area far out in the ocean

2. Which definition best describes '**tourists**'?
   a. visitors who go to see interesting places
   b. a kind of fisherman

B A Tourist Center. Complete the paragraph with the words in the box. Then answer the questions.

culture	environment	pollution	tourism

(1) _____ is the business of bringing visitors to an area. However, both benefits and problems come with tourists. Tourism can affect the (2) _____, or nature, of a place. It can increase (3) _____ by making the area unclean and noisy. Tourism can also affect the (4) _____ of a group of people. It can make them forget their traditions and history.

1. What are some of the benefits of tourism? _____

2. What are some of the problems with tourism? _____

4. _____

1. _____

5. _____

2. _____

A Fishing Port

3. _____

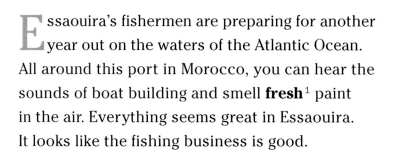

Essaouira's fishermen are preparing for another year out on the waters of the Atlantic Ocean. All around this port in Morocco, you can hear the sounds of boat building and smell **fresh**[1] paint in the air. Everything seems great in Essaouira. It looks like the fishing business is good.

---

[1] **fresh:** new

CD 1, Track 07

But in reality, things are not very good here. In Essaouira, fishing is no longer such a good job. The number of fish that the fishermen catch has gone down in recent years. Some of the fishing work has gone away; it's moved to the south of Morocco. The size of the boats is one of the biggest problems. The small boats which leave this port can't **compete with**[2] the big fishing boats from other places. Those big boats, or trawlers, can simply catch more fish.

One fisherman explains the difficulties of life as a fisherman in Essaouira. He says that there's not a lot of work, and sometimes there's no work at all: "The life of a fisherman now is hard," he says. "Sometimes you work for one day; then you don't work for two days. Then you work for one week; then no work for fifteen days." The fishing industry here is trying to **survive**,[3] but it's very difficult. However, now there's new hope for the town of Essaouira.

---

[2] **compete with:** try to do better than
[3] **survive:** continue to exist

Predict

Write definitions for the following expressions: 'breadwinner' and 'tourist boom'. Then scan pages 9 and 10 to compare your definitions with those in the reader.

Recently, this town has found a new **breadwinner**;[4] tourism. Many people think that this breadwinner will be the future of Essaouira.

Last year, thousands of tourists visited Essaouira from all over the world. This tourism has brought hope and money to the town. Can tourism bring more money to the village than fishing? Does it hold the future of this old fishing village?

---

[4] **breadwinner:** main person or business that makes money

UNION

For now, no one can be certain. However, tourism is not new here. Essaouira's first **tourist boom**[5] was in the 1960s. Rock stars and people from many different cultures visited the village. They wanted to walk in its little streets, see the port and enjoy its beauty. But then tourism went away and the people had to depend more on fishing again.

Now, the small town is trying to bring in tourists again. The people of Essaouira worry that perhaps the fishing industry is dying. They want a different way to make money, perhaps an easier way. Their plan is working well – tourism is growing fast here. Since 1996, tourism in Essaouira has increased by more than 300 percent!

---

[5]**tourist boom:** successful time for tourist businesses

It's not difficult to see why visitors like the village. It's very beautiful, and it's also very old. There's also a lot of history there. Essaouira's 'medina', or old town center, was built in the 1700s. It was recently put on **UNESCO's World Heritage List**[6]. It's a place where visitors can go back in time to a different world.

---

[6]**UNESCO World Heritage List:** a list of important cultural places in the world chosen by the United Nations Educational, Scientific, and Cultural Organization (UNESCO)

Essaouira now has a very good chance to develop tourism and help its economy. However tourism can also bring changes and problems with it. Sometimes, when tourism increases, the economy grows too quickly. This can cause problems for the local culture. The local environment can become worse because of pollution, as well.

It's going to be important for this village not to **sell out**[7] its people, culture and environment. It's also going to be important that the tourist industry doesn't grow too quickly.

---

[7]**sell out:** give away something valuable for money (negative meaning)

The people who are developing tourism in Essaouira say that **conservation**[8] is very important to them. However, for the people of the village there are still questions about water, land use and pollution. They want a business that makes money, but they also know that they have to be very careful. They know that they can't allow tourism to grow without some control.

---

[8]**conservation:** keeping the environment clean

What do you think?

1. Should Essaouira increase tourism?

2. Why or why not?

3. What should they do to keep their culture and traditions safe?

Is fishing now part of Essaouira's past? Maybe. Perhaps now this quiet fishing port has a chance to make a new life for itself; a life for the future.

The people of Essaouira now have to make some very important decisions. Will they be able to control the pollution? Will they be able to save the environment? Will they choose well? No one knows. The people of Essaouira do know one thing; what they do now is important. The future of their beautiful little village for tomorrow may depend on the decisions they make today.

After You Read

1. The word 'great' on page 4 can be replaced by:
   A. enjoy
   B. noisy
   C. busy
   D. fine

2. Each is a problem for the fishermen of Essaouira EXCEPT:
   A. Their boats are too small.
   B. There are too few fish.
   C. They are getting ready.
   D. They can't compete with trawlers.

3. Sometimes fishermen don't have _____ work for 15 days.
   A. any
   B. no
   C. one
   D. a

4. What is a good heading for page 10?
   A. Rock Star Coming to Essaouira
   B. Tourism Brings Hope and Money
   C. Morocco Loves Essaouira
   D. Too Many Tourists

5. In paragraph 2 on page 10, 'they' refers to:
   A. people from different cultures
   B. tourists in Essaouira
   C. rock stars
   D. the people of Essaouira

6. According to the paragraph on page 13 Essaouira is a _____ and _____ town.
   A. beautiful, historic
   B. different, historic
   C. famous, medina
   D. great, safe

7. What does 'it' refer to in 'it was recently' on page 13?
   A. tourism
   B. the medina
   C. Essaouira
   D. UNESCO

8. What is one reason Essaouira has a good chance to develop tourism?
   A. People are interested in the old town center
   B. The environment is not safe
   C. Tourists can meet fishermen
   D. The small boats are good for tourists

9. The best heading for page 16 is:
   A. Tourism Helps Local Culture
   B. Water Pollution
   C. Conservation Begins with Tourism
   D. Tourism without Control May Be Bad

10. What does 'past' mean on page 19?
   A. story
   B. history
   C. environment
   D. tourism

11. What is the purpose of this story?
   A. to show that fishermen have problems
   B. to teach that tourism is good
   C. to teach that conservation is important
   D. to tell about an old town trying to make a new life

What's happening to Maui?

Hawaii is a collection of six small islands near the center of the Pacific Ocean. It is almost always warm in Hawaii, so millions of tourists visit the islands each year. All of the islands are beautiful, but Maui is especially beautiful. As a result, it is one of the tourists' favorite places to visit. This island alone receives more than two million tourists every year.

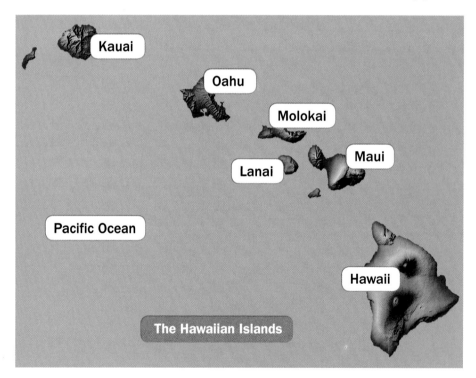

Kauai

Oahu

Molokai

Maui

Lanai

Pacific Ocean

Hawaii

The Hawaiian Islands

For many years, the main business and form of trade in Maui was farming. However, a tourist boom began in the 1960s. Since then, tourism has become the most important industry on the island.

sand

ocean

beach

The sand on Maui's beaches can be different colors.

Most tourists visit Maui because of the beaches. They are especially interesting because the sand in some places is white and in other places it can seem to be black, red or even green.

Unfortunately, Maui's travel industry does have some serious problems. First of all, the two million tourists who visit the island each year need somewhere to stay. Therefore, land developers have built many large buildings in some of the most beautiful areas. Many of them are not very nice to look at. The buildings have also had a bad effect on the environment and there has been an increase in air and water pollution. Conservation groups have tried, but they are not able to slow this growth.

In addition, tourists need people to care for them. Therefore, more people are now living on the island all year round. In the 1960s, the number of people living on Maui was about 40,000. Today it is almost 140,000!

The traditional Hawaiian culture is now no longer easy to find. Some old villages no longer exist. The people of Maui must make some important decisions for their future. They must decide how to save their island and keep tourists happy at the same time.

CD 1, Track 08

Word Count: 316
Time: _____

Vocabulary List

boat building (2, 4)

boom (7, 10)

breadwinner (7, 9)

compete with (6)

conservation (16)

culture (3, 10, 14, 16)

environment (3, 14, 19)

fish (2, 6)

fishermen (2, 4, 6)

fishing boat (2, 6)

fresh (4)

pollution (3, 14, 16, 19)

port (2, 3, 4, 6, 10, 19)

sell out (14)

survive (6)

tourism (3, 9, 10, 14, 16)

tourist (2, 9, 10)

village (2, 9, 10, 13, 14, 16, 19)